On A Wing and A Wish

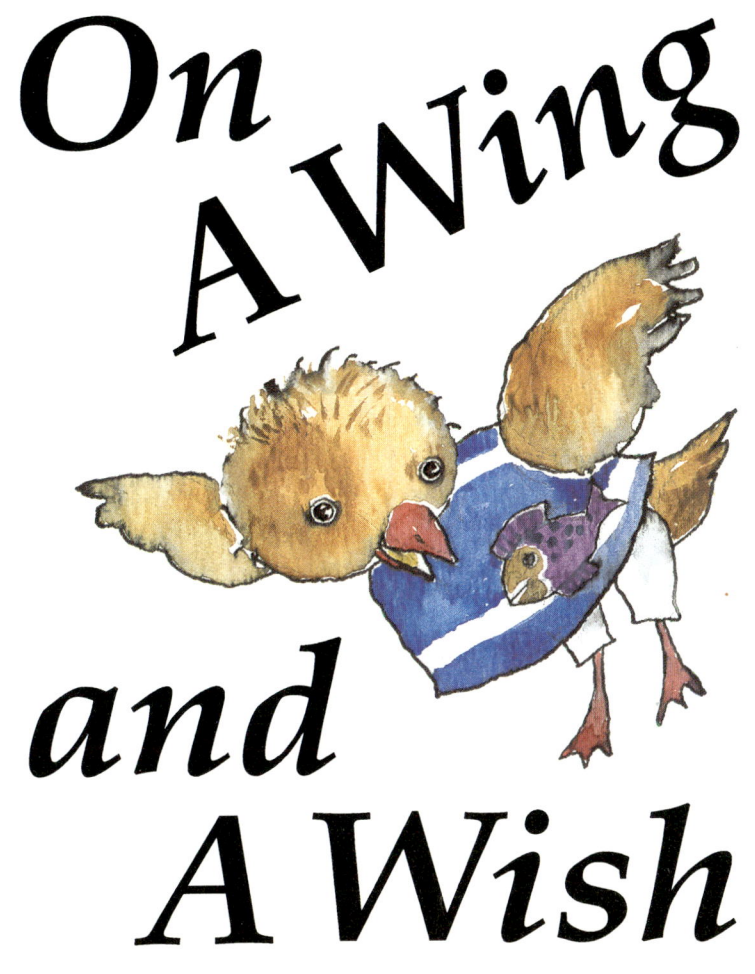

Salt Water Bird Rhymes

by Al Pittman

illustrated by Veselina Tomova

Breakwater Books
100 Water Street
P.O. Box 2188
St. John's, Newfoundland, Canada
A1C 6E6

The Publisher gratefully acknowledges the support of The Canada Council which has helped make this publication possible.

The Publisher acknowledges the financial contribution of the Cultural Affairs Division of the Department of Culture, Recreation and Youth, Government of Newfoundland and Labrador, which has helped make this publication possible.

Canadian Cataloguing in Publication Data

Pittman, Al, 1940-
   On a wing and a wish
   Poems.

ISBN 0-920911-64-1
   1. Birds — Newfoundland — Juvenile Poetry. 2. Children's poetry, Canadian (English) *Veselina Tomova II. Title.

PS8531.I7706 1989 jC811'.54 C89-098646-0
PZ8.3.P570n 1989

Copyright ©1992 Al Pittman
Veselina Tomova
ALL RIGHTS RESERVED. No part of this work covered by copyrights hereon may be reproduced or used in any form or by any means—graphic, electronic or mechanical—without the prior written permission of the publisher. Any request for photocopying, recording taping or information storage and retrieval systems of any part of this book shall be directed in writing to the Canadian Reprography Collective, 370 Adelaide Street West, Suite M1, Toronto, Ontario M5V 1S5.

*For Kyran and Emily
with love*

Other books for children by Al Pittman

Down by Jim Long's Stage: Rhymes for Children and Young Fish
illustrated by Pam Hall
(Breakwater, 1977)

One Wonderful Fine Day for a Sculpin Named Sam
illustrated by Shawn Steffler
(Breakwater, 1983)

*Have you ever sailed in the salt sea sky,
Or ever wished you could?*

*Oh, wouldn't it be wonderful.
Oh, wouldn't it be good
To whirl and swirl and swing about
Without a care or sorrow,
Without a care about today
Much less about tomorrow.*

*And wouldn't it be heavenly
Not to be confined
As fish and other creatures are—
People and their kind.*

*Oh, you might think so,
And be quite right
To wish yourself as free
As any bird who ever sailed
The sky above the sea.*

*But do be careful with your dreams
(With what you wish for and desire)
For no matter how high you are able to fly,
Up will always be higher.*

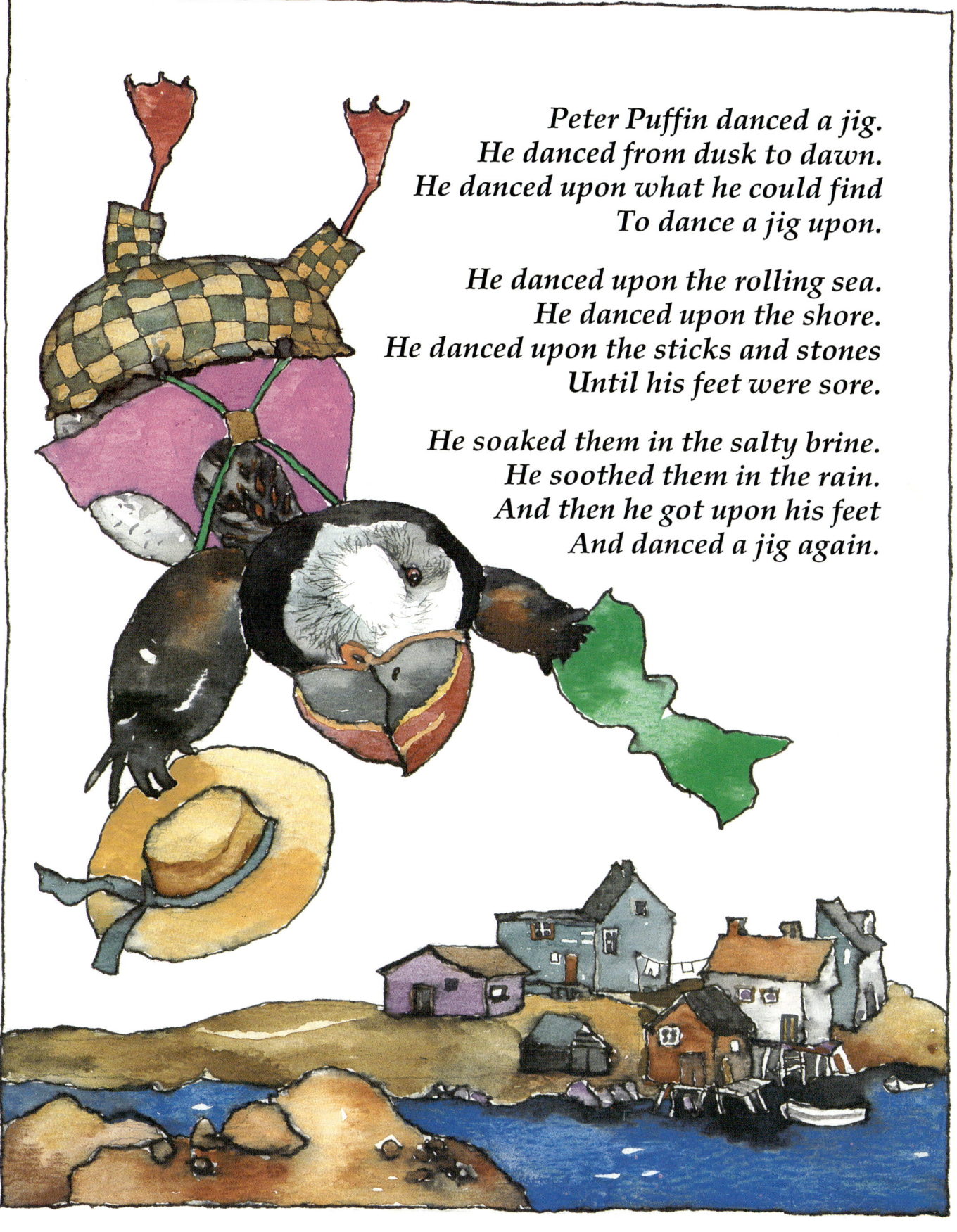

Peter Puffin danced a jig.
He danced from dusk to dawn.
He danced upon what he could find
To dance a jig upon.

He danced upon the rolling sea.
He danced upon the shore.
He danced upon the sticks and stones
Until his feet were sore.

He soaked them in the salty brine.
He soothed them in the rain.
And then he got upon his feet
And danced a jig again.

Sally Seagull's fondest wish
Was to have a meal that wasn't fish.

At night asleep she'd dream of things
Like hot dogs, french fries, onion rings.

She'd dream of pizzas and donairs,
Of lemon pies and rich éclairs.

By dreaming she'd fulfill her wish
And feast on every food but fish.

Alas, poor Sally, by and by,
Had to dream that she could fly.

Black Jack Saddleback
A grumpy gull was he.
He lived alone upon a ledge
That overlooked the sea.

He sat upon that ledge all day
And scowled at passers-by.
For breakfast he had frankum gum
For supper seaweed pie.

Gary Gannett was a wise old bird.
He soared in the sky all day.

He soared and he soared
And he never got bored.

And he never had nothing to say.

*A hound who found
In Paradise Sound
An elegant hound named Heather
Thought she was the most heavenly sight
He'd seen in foggy weather.*

*In Paradise Sound
The hounds abound
In fair and foggy weather
But she was the first he'd ever seen
Dressed up in fine mink feather.*

Sharon Shag had The Hag.
Almost every night
She'd lie awake for hours
Paralysed with fright.

"There's no such thing as an Old Hag!"
Sharon's mother said.
"That's just some silly notion
You've got inside your head."

From that time on, she slept quite well.
Each night passed like the other.
She slept in peace, because The Hag
Was haunting Sharon's mother.

One warm and windy day in Spring
While fooling around in flight
Henry Hound got clobbered
In a collision with a kite.

All tattered and torn
He got nothing but scorn
As he flapped from place to place
Claiming he had been attacked
By a bird from outer space.

Harold Hagdown wore blue serge
And chewed seaweed tobacco.
He was so behind the times
The youngsters thought him whacko.

Harold, he got all dressed up
And off to the time did stroll.
He danced the lancers and the reel
But he cursed the rock and roll.

A crowd of Mother Carey's chicks
Went skipping in the sky
And the song they sang while skipping
Was enough to make you cry.

"Berries in the marshes
Berries on the hill
Berries in the boggy bog
Pick them where you will.

Partridge berry jam
Bakeapple pie
Billy got a belly ache
And so have I."

*A gill bird named Gail
Was sure she could sing
Like a robin, a wren, or a sparrow.*

*In sun, rain, or hail
All day on the wing
She'd squawk like a squeaky wheelbarrow.*

*Poor old batty Bernard Bawk
Thought he was the last great auk.*

*Like an auk he'd try to walk.
Like an auk he'd try to talk.*

*If he was told he was just a bawk
He'd stand and stare and balk and squawk.*

*And that's why other birds would gawk
At poor old batty Bernard Bawk.*

Silly Billy Bullbird
While sound asleep in bed
Dreamt he did a somersault
And landed on his head.

When he woke up next morning
He got a big surprise.
A hundred thousand starfish
Swam before his eyes.

Sandy, a piper of Scottish descent,
Played on the pipes all night.

He kept his neighbours wide awake
While he played to his own delight.

***He played** The Flowers of Edinburgh*
***And he played** The Castle Keep.*

At sunrise he played Auld Lang Syne
Then quit and went to sleep.

*Terrible Terrence was a terrible turr.
A tyrant turr was he.
The roughest, toughest, bulliest bird
That ever went to sea.*

*Out on The Funks he ruled and reigned
Like some almighty lord
Until the other turrs rebelled
And threw him overboard.*

*Now Terrence lives in exile
All alone but quite content
Because he's oh so happy,
To have no one to torment.*

*Idle Tommy Tickleace
On an idle day
Said to Peggy Puffin
"How'd ya like to play?"*

*"You get lost!" said Peggy
"You'll tickle me no more.
I don't like being tickled
Into laughing 'til I'm sore."*

*A razor-bill named Rachel
Complained of such a cramp
She walked the shore the whole night long
By the light of the lighthouse lamp.*

*She wouldn't call the doctor.
She wouldn't call the nurse.
She just went on complaining
'Til her husband called the hearse.*

*Young Kent Kittiwake
Had one heroic notion.
He thought he could get rid of crime
In the sky above the ocean.*

*Whenever he thought 'trouble'
In secret he would say
"This is a job for Superbird!
Up! Up! And Away!"*

*His x-ray vision on the blink
Over ice-bergs high
He'd soar in search of phone booths
On sidewalks in the sky.*

*While crimes went undetected
And trouble spread around
Young Kent would keep on looking
For what could not be found.*

*When he was all worn out
He'd try hard not to cry
While wishing he could find, just once,
That phone booth in the sky.*

Sherman Shag, the shaggiest shag
Of the shags out on Shag Rocks
Had no use for instruments
For radar, maps, or clocks.

Sherman lived forlorn, alone.
He couldn't find a mate.
But he thought for sure he'd find one
If he went to Twillingate.

Without a compass or a chart
He took off one dark night.
Now he lives forlorn, alone,
In far off South East Bight.

A pigeon called Paul
Got caught in a squall
On his way across Notre Dame Bay.

The wind and the snow
Blew high and blew low
And poor Paul blew every which way.

Elsie Eider and Lucy Loo
While swimming side by side
Wondered which of them would be
The first to be a bride.

Elsie thought that she'd be first
And Lucy thought that she'd be.
And neither of them thought at all
That neither of them need be.

Steve Stearin one day
While out on the bay
Picked up some rather nice offal.

He could hardly wait
To sit down to a plate
And devour it all by the jaw-full.

So slimy and pink
With such a fine stink
He thought he would die if he couldn't.

So home he did fly
With a gleam in his eye
And asked his good wife if she wouldn't.

As though it were duff
She seasoned the stuff
And served up a goodly sized maw-full.

Steve in his haste
Gulped down the first taste
And declared "This offal is awful!"

Steve Stearin one day
While out on the bay
Picked up some rather nice offal.

He could hardly wait
To sit down to a plate
And devour it all by the jaw-full.

So slimy and pink
With such a fine stink
He thought he would die if he couldn't.

So home he did fly
With a gleam in his eye
And asked his good wife if she wouldn't.

As though it were duff
She seasoned the stuff
And served up a goodly sized maw-full.

Steve in his haste
Gulped down the first taste
And declared "This offal is awful!"

Oswald Osprey high on a cliff
As high as high can be
Wondered what it would be like
To live beneath the sea.

What would you do but swim around
And stay wet all your life.
And Yuk! A fish would have to have
A fish to be his wife.

It can't be very nice, he thought,
To never ever fly
And never ever touch a cloud
And never know the sky.

I think I'd rather be a bird
Than any kind of fish
And since I am, and I am me,
I've nothing more to wish.

Following is a list of coastal birds who inhabit the pages of *On a Wing and a Wish*. The names in the left column are those I believe to be the most commonly used in Newfoundland, and hence the names used in the rhymes. The names in the right column are those which identify the same birds in *The Birds of Newfoundland* by Harold S. Peters and Thomas D. Burleigh, illustrated by Roger Tory Peterson, and published by the Department of Natural Resources, Government of Newfoundland and Labrador, in 1951. The names in brackets are alternate names by which these birds are known locally.

Bawk	Greater Shearwater (Hagdown)
Bullbird	Common Dovekie (Ice-bird)
Eider	Northern Common Eider
Gannet	Gannet
Gill Bird	Northern Phalarope (Gale Bird)
Great Auk	Great Auk (Penguin) - Extinct
Hagdown	Sooty Shearwater (Hag)
Hound	Oldsquaw (Duck)
Kittiwake	Atlantic Black-legged Kittiwake (Tickleace)
Loo	Greater Common Loon
Mother Carey's Chick	Northern Leach's Petrel (Storm Petrel)
Osprey	American Osprey (Fish-hawk)
Pigeon	Southern Black Guillemot (Sea Pigeon)
Puffin	Atlantic Common Puffin (Sea Parrot)
Razor-bill	Northern Razor-bill (Tinker)
Saddle-back	Great Black-backed Gull
Sandpiper	Spotted Sandpiper (Beachy Bird)
Seagull	American Herring Gull (Bluey)
Shag	Atlantic Common Cormorant
Stearin	Northern Common Tern (Paytrick)
Tickleace	Atlantic Black-legged Kittiwake (Kittiwake)
Turr	Atlantic Common Murre (Baccalieu Bird)